The Joy of the LORD is My STRENGTH

Michael Soppeland

ISBN 978-1-64140-475-4 (paperback)
ISBN 978-1-64140-476-1 (digital)

Copyright © 2018 by Michael Soppeland

All rights reserved. No part of this publication may be reproduced, distributed, or transmitted in any form or by any means, including photocopying, recording, or other electronic or mechanical methods without the prior written permission of the publisher. For permission requests, solicit the publisher via the address below.

Christian Faith Publishing, Inc.
832 Park Avenue
Meadville, PA 16335
www.christianfaithpublishing.com

Unless otherwise noted. (In one chapter I quote from the NAS).
New American Standard
All Scripture quotations are from the Revised Standard Version of the Bible, Thomas Nelson Inc. (Nashville, Camden, New York, 1972).

Printed in the United States of America

I dedicate this book to my sister, Nancy, and my two brothers, Jim and Paul. Their love, encouragement, and support for me have been wonderful and so appreciated.

Foreword

In my years as a youth and family pastor in a large church, I often went to workshops and seminars on the needs and interests of young people. I would also exchange ideas and implement new ways for the young folks to experience the love and grace of God in their lives.

In one of my conversations with a Methodist pastor, he told me they had a bulletin board in their youth room. The high schoolers would tack up names of people who had gone from friends to couples. *Mary* and *John* would be written with a heart around their names. The interesting conversation with this pastor was that if the popular song of the week or month was about true love and finding the person of your dreams, there would be several names on the board. If the song for a time was about the sadness of breaking up or the loss of true love, the names would be taken down. The romance or lack of it depended on the top forty songs of the week.

Music has nearly always influenced the behavior of people. Musicians and songwriters are often the best psychologists, sociologists, and theologians. If a person wants to memorize a particular line from poetry or a song or Scripture, they put it to music. *"Abcdefghijklmnop . . ."* is one example. Even those who can't "carry a tune in a bucket" sing in the car or the shower. The poet and musician Bob Dylan has received the Nobel Prize in Literature because of the philosophical depth of his music.

I began each chapter with a song from a variety of genres and eras, though most are Christian. They are words that tell a story, paint a picture, express feelings, or describe an emotion. The writer has either experienced about what they are writing or seen someone else go through the joy or despair of an incident in life. The book is meant to be descriptive, not prescriptive.

The title comes from the book of Nehemiah in the Old Testament. It is the result of the despair of the Israelites leading to the joy of hope in God. In their journey of life, the trials and challenges took a toll. But for those who stayed faithful and strong, the reward was joy and strength.

My hope is that the reader would find a sense of grace and hope in the songs I have chosen and the meaning that is given. There are several different ways to understand words: what a person is experiencing now, what they experienced yesterday, and what they hope to experience tomorrow. We are also affected by what we believe about life, death, God, and faith. May you be blessed and encouraged that you are not alone in this life and the stuff you have lived through can make you a stronger and better-rounded person. For after all is said and done, we are simply ordinary people on a journey. And for me, it is the joy of God's great love that gives me strength.

Chapter One

Just Ordinary

"Ordinary Man"[1]

1. In between the doubts and the dreamin'
Comes my humble quest for a plan
I've been out there hoverin' by
Don't forget to pull me in sometimes.
Will you be with me as I make my journey
Through the labyrinth of time?
And I'm still waitin' for the good Lord
To show me the way, babe.

Chorus: This is who you see, this is who I am.
Please forgive me if I fall sometimes,
Just an ordinary man.

2. Will my reckless courage invite you
To become my clever companion?
Madly in love and in love with the madness,
Get ready to run baby.

This is who you see, this is who I am.
Please forgive me if I fall sometimes,
Just an ordinary man.

3. Enjoyin' the ride
Savor the simple pleasure
With you by my side.

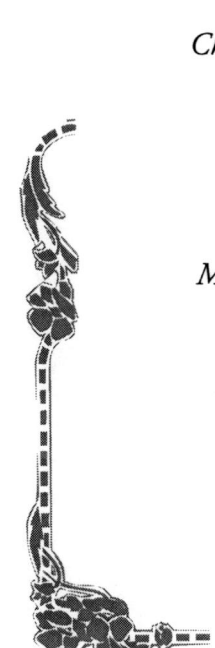

It was a cloudy day with intermittent rain showers. I was working in my office on sermons for the coming Sunday and Wednesday Lenten services. On my CD was playing *The Very Best of the Doobie Brothers*. I didn't recognize the last song on the second CD of the set, so I stopped what I was doing and turned to listen. I heard the words *ordinary man*.

That's it, I thought. *That's me. That's what I feel like . . . and I like it.* I got up and restarted the song. While not all the words applied, certainly most of them did, especially the chorus: "This is who you see, this is who I am. Please forgive me if I fall sometimes, just an ordinary man."

I had wondered for years if an ordinary man was something a person was granted. Did one have to work toward it? What were the qualifications? What were the people whom I most admired in life doing to make them my examples and inspiration? What's wrong with being ordinary?

I have worked in the world of religion and faith all my adult life. And I have found that most religious people have a difficult time truly believing in a God who genuinely and truly loves them unconditionally. In all the Bible studies that I have attended or led, there are several people who bring up issues of not being good enough and how that has affected their outlook on life and their relationships. It is usually, first of all, the kind of home in which they were raised. And then, second, it is the way they were viewed by their church or place of worship and what and how they were taught about God. There is a difference between religion and faith. It is important to separate those two.

Being ordinary is often how we view our accomplishments. Every new year that comes, we vow to do something or give up something that is keeping us from being happy. Someone has said, "A New Year's resolution is something that goes in one year and out the other." A better way of approaching the new year is to say, "Every year, I make a resolution to change myself. This year, I'm making a resolution to be myself."

Several years ago, the late Charles Schulz wrote a *Peanuts* cartoon strip for December 31 that had Snoopy think to himself, *So this is the last day of the year. Another complete year gone by and what have I accomplished this year that I haven't accomplished every other year? Nothing!*

He smiles and thinks to himself, *How consistent can you get?*

Even if a person doesn't believe in a supreme being who created the universe, that person still wrestles with self-worth, self-love, and self-acceptance. Those characteristics and others are no respecter of persons. They are equal opportunity struggles. There seems to be something at the very core of our being and soul that wants to be an important part of the world, yet we think that we can't or won't find our place and purpose in it unless we change who we are. For those of us who are Christians, we are encouraged to be consistently transformed into the image of Christ. We understand that in order for us to be "good" Christians, we must live our lives based on the adage "What would Jesus do?" But if we take that phrase to its logical end, we will be driven crazy trying to adapt who Jesus was in the New Testament in terms of His personality to how we live today. Questions such as "Would Jesus own a gun?" and "Would Jesus own property and hold a job?" and "Would Jesus be a Democrat or a Republican?" I was told by a very well-meaning Christian that it is a sin to wear red. When I asked why, her response was that red is the devil's color. She never did explain where she got that. When I was in my twenties, I was told that Christians don't have long hair. I had long hair and was a Christian. Now what? I could have told those folks that I was trying to be like Jesus. I also wore sandals that we called Jesus's shoes. There must be more to it than that. There must be additional thoughts that we are missing if we think that God wants to change the "who" of who we are.

There is a science film from 1977 titled *The Powers of Ten*.[2] It opens with a close-up of a young couple spreading out a picnic blanket in Chicago's Grant Park. Every ten seconds, the camera pulls back, increasing the distance from the now-sleeping man by the power of ten. The camera pulls back a meter, then ten meters, then one hundred meters, and so on. Within a few seconds, Grant Park has been reduced to a small green patch. Next, Chicago disappears as you see all of the United States. Within a couple of minutes, the picture is such that you only see the outer limits of the Milky Way

Galaxy. The film is a reminder of how small we are compared to the huge size of the universe.

Astronomers have found an empty big place in the universe. It is a massive hole, nearly a billion light-years across. Inside this hole, there are no planets or stars. It is between six and ten billion light-years away from earth. Our brains simply cannot comprehend a hole that huge. Blaise Pascal, a mathematician and philosopher, called the human heart an infinite abyss.

In Psalms chapter 8, it says, "When I consider your heavens, the work of your fingers, the moon and the stars, which you have set in place, what is humankind that you are mindful of them, human beings that you care for them?" This universe is so huge; why should God care about us at all? There are so many of us to love, over six and a half billion. But there is a truth here. The more you know about a subject, any subject, the less you think in terms of the universal or the general and the more you think in terms of the specific or the individual.

Most of us know nothing about what goes on under the hood of a car. Author John Ortberg says this: "If my car breaks down, I sometimes look under the hood. I have no idea why I'm doing this. If under the hood there were a giant ON-OFF switch turned to the 'Off' position, I would have some idea what to do . . ."[3]

If I look under the hood of my 1970 Chevrolet Impala, I know what goes where and what needs fixing. A mechanic looks under the hood, especially of cars built in the last few decades, but he doesn't see a mass of metal, wires, and hoses. From the computer, he knows exactly what's wrong and where and how to fix it. He understands the car's individual parts.

God knows every single person in the world by name. And your name is important to God and to you. It helps define who you are. It gives you recognition among the other people in the world. God knows every Israeli and Palestinian. He knows every child in Zambia and South Africa. Every hair on the head of someone from Thailand and India God knows.

Early in the computer years, many studies were being done to gauge the efficiency of those computers on learning. I remember reading about one of those studies in a middle school in California. Computers were being given to the school, but they were off-limits to the special education youth to minimize the risk of damage. One of the teachers made a fuss about it, so the policy was reversed.

In one semester, some of those special education students learned more than in the preceding ten years. One boy named Raymond had every problem in the book: a dysfunctional homelife, bad eyesight, and extreme shyness. In that one semester, he caught up seven years in his math scores.

When he was asked how it was that he did so wonderfully, he said, "Well, you see, all the kids here call me retard. The computer calls me Raymond."

His name and being called by his name, even by the computer, was so important to him that he began to excel academically.

In Martin Luther's *Small Catechism*, he gives a meaning to the first section (article) of the Apostles' Creed. It says, "I believe that God has created me and all that exists; that God has given me and still sustains my body and soul."[4]

Is the universe friendly? Very much so! Did God make it? Yes. Is it OK to be ordinary? Absolutely. In this age of self-help books and inspirational speakers, I have liked the thought that I am a nobody. I am not rich or famous or well-known. I do what millions and millions of people do every day: get up, go to work of some sort, and attempt to make sense of the world. We are on a journey. It's called life. And that gives me joy. And I find my strength in that joy.

---

[1] Bob Bangerter, Michael Ruff, and Neida Bequette, "Ordinary Man," sung by the Doobie Brothers (BMI/Ruffmix Music, 2000).
[2] Charles Eames and Ray, *The Powers of Ten*, based on *Cosmic View* by Kees Boeke (distributed by IBM, 1977).
[3] John Ortberg, *When the Game Is Over It All Goes Back in the Box* (Grand Rapids, MI: Zondervan Publishing, 2009).
[4] Martin Luther, *The Book of Concord* (Fortress Press, Philadelphia, PA: Fourteenth Printing 1981, pg. 345).

Chapter Two

The Power of Love

"What Becomes of the Brokenhearted?"[1]

*1. As I walk this land of broken dreams
I have visions of many things
But happiness is just an illusion
Filled with sadness and confusion*

*Chorus: What becomes of the brokenhearted
Who had love that's now departed?
I know I've got to find
Some kind of peace of mind, maybe.*

*2. If roots of love grow all around
But for me they come tumblin' down
Every day heartaches grow a little stronger
I can't stand this pain much longer*

*3. I walk in shadows searching for light
Cold and alone no comfort in sight
Hopin' and prayin' for someone to care
Always movin' and goin' nowhere*

*4. I'm searchin' though I don't succeed
But someone's love there's a growin' need
All is lost there's no place for beginning
All that's left is an unhappy ending*

THE JOY OF THE LORD IS MY STRENGTH

This song from the midsixties sung by Jimmy Ruffin really addresses the power of love and its effect on the soul. In an ordinary human, is the love of another so important to my feelings of value that it can have devastating effects for years and years? While I do not profess to be a psychologist or therapist, based on my experiences of people, the answer is a definite yes. I have in recent years used the phrase of having someone cheering for you.

Sports figures feel it often. At a professional event, a mixture of flashing and colored lights brighten the arena, and deep, resonating sounds of music play as each participant is introduced. The crowd yells and screams their names in joy and appreciation as each one is announced. They are standing on their feet and clapping as a spotlight is shone on the image running or skating onto the area of competition. It is exhilarating, both for the fan and the player. The atmosphere is, as is often said, electric.

Every morning, when a person gets out of bed, how would it feel if there were ten thousand people ready and willing—after one gets up and showers, that is—to yell their name and cheer them on for the day, to let them know that they are loved and that there is a whole bunch of folks wanting them to do their best and have a wonderful and meaningful day? That person would want to do their best on the job. They would want to find their sense of place in the world. They would better understand themselves and the world in which they live. They would be more loving and caring to those with whom they live. The phrase in the song "hopin' and prayin' for someone to care, always movin' and goin' nowhere" is truly the definition of love. To say to someone "I deeply care about you and what you do" is the same or nearly the same as saying "I love you." *Love* is an action word. As we are told over and over again, it is not a feeling, though wonderful when it is.

In the play and movie *Fiddler on the Roof*,[2] there is a conversation between the main character, Tevye, and his wife, Golda.

> Tevye: "Do you love me?"
> Golda: "Do I what?"

After a few lines of dialogue, Tevye persists.

Tevye: "Golda, I'm asking you a question, do you love me?"
Golda: "You're a fool!"
Tevye: "I know. But do you love me?"
Golda: "Do I love you? For twenty-five years, I've washed your clothes, cooked your meals, cleaned your house, given you children, milked the cows. After twenty-five years, why talk about love now?"

Tevye wants to hear Golda tell him. He is asking if she feels love for him. Is there emotion in her commitment to him? Is there passion? Will she hold his hand and hug him?

Some would take advantage of unconditional love. Some would sin that grace may abound. Some would abuse the power that that kind of love would give them. But I believe a huge majority would be more adventurous, more entrepreneurial, more willing to take calculated risks, and more willing to accept failure and continue to look forward. Deeper than the fear of failure is the fear of not being loved by anyone. If we know that there is someone we can trust to pick us up when we fall or stumble in life, we will be much more willing to accept the challenges that we all face. It's called unconditional love. It's a love that is learned early in life.

A person growing up in an abusive home is more likely to abuse their own children. It is all they know about compassion and kindness. On the other hand, a person raised in a tender and affirming environment will carry that through into their own family and offspring. Children are good recorders of life, but they aren't able to interpret what happens. They read body language and behavior more than the spoken word.

A friend of mine commented to me that in his church, as a young person, the unspoken message was that everyone needed to be happy because that is how we would prove that the gospel was real. It was an unspoken agreement. The language addressing that approach was indirect and never articulated.

One example of broken love and then fulfilled love is the story of Jacob in Genesis 29. Jacob is single and walking through an area known as Haran. He comes upon a group of shepherds and finds out that the owner of the sheep is his uncle, Laban. They have brought their flock to a watering hole. As they are talking with each other, Rachel, his cousin, a shepherdess, is bringing her sheep to also get a drink. Jacob is smitten with Rachel, and when Rachel returns, she tells her dad about Jacob. Laban is overjoyed that his nephew has come and invites Jacob to stay. Jacob remains a month with the family, and eventually Laban asks him what he wants for wages as he has been working during this time. Jacob asks Laban if he could have Rachel as his wife. When Laban agrees, Jacob tells him he will stay and work for seven years just to be able to marry Rachel. In verse 20, we read, "So Jacob served seven years for Rachel and they seemed to him but a few days because of his love for her."

When the seven years are up, Laban "gives him" secretly at night his oldest daughter, Leah. When Jacob finds out the next morning, he is outraged at his uncle. Laban admits that the rules are that the oldest has to marry first. Jacob is told that he can have Rachel after a week of celebrating his marriage to Leah. Jacob, however, works for another seven years without wages, only room and board.

I wonder what Jacob was thinking after finding out he had been deceived by his own uncle. Was this some kind of trick? Fourteen years went by before the marriage was truly final. The debt was paid.

Jacob lived out the words "movin' and goin' nowhere." That means that the person is active and living life, but there is that nagging feeling of despair and discouragement that one can't ignore. It is where we get the term "running on a treadmill." I have walked and jogged on a treadmill. Even with dials and digital numbers and screens in front of me, I would rather exercise outdoors. Why? Because on a machine, after the mileage gauge tells me I have gone two miles, I am still in the same physical spot I was in thirty minutes prior. I have gone nowhere. My heart rate is up to 120 beats per minute, but I am still stuck where I started. As the song states, "What becomes of the brokenhearted who had love that's now departed?"

Why do we call departed love pain? What hurts? If I have a headache, everyone understands where the pain is located. But a broken heart . . . We transplant hearts. And I have read that those transplanted hearts into a new body seem to change the recipient of that heart. The reasons are not totally clear. Perhaps it is the result of having the heart surgery in the first place, a close call with death, the idea that without it, that person would die. Whatever the reason, if one has a heart that is broken, it usually refers to love lost, a betrayal. It is something we feel in the soul. It could be that there is not a lot of difference between love and hate. One can turn to the other in a matter of moments.

As a pastor officiating at a funeral, I often have a prayer with the family just prior to entering the sanctuary for the service. It is at that time that I remind them that there is a price to pay for loving someone. And that price is that we miss them when they are gone. How tragic it would be to go through life not loving anyone and never being loved by anyone. The upside of grieving, though there may be unresolved guilt about words that were spoken or not spoken to the loved one, is that sadness comes to those who genuinely love and miss that person, and that in itself shows they meant something to you.

The psalmist in many places says that it is the love of the Lord that supports me. And in Psalms 34:18, we read, "The Lord is near to the broken-hearted, and saves the crushed in spirit." Finding those love answers is a part of being an ordinary person and living in the joy of the Lord.

---

[1] "What Becomes of the Brokenhearted?" sung by Jimmy Ruffin, written by James Dean, Paul Riser, and William Weatherspoon (Soul Records, 1966).
[2] Sholem Aleichem. Library of Yiddish classics. Written between 1894 and 1914.

Chapter Three

Pursuing Happiness

"Happy"[1]

It might seem crazy what I'm about to say
Sunshine she's here you can take a break
I'm a hot air balloon that could go to space
With the air like I don't care baby by the way

Chorus: Because I'm happy
Clap along if you feel like a room without a roof
Because I'm happy
Clap along it you feel like happiness is the truth
Because I'm happy
Clap along if you know what happiness is to you
Because I'm happy
Clap along if you feel like that's what you wanna do

Here comes bad news talking this and that
Well gimme all you got and don't hold back
Well I should probably warn you I'll be just fine
No offense to you, don't waste your time, here's why

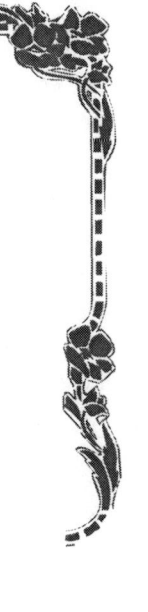

This catchy little song hit number one in 2013. It is the theme song to an animated movie called *Despicable Me 2* and sung by Pharrell Williams. It could be taken as philosophical. And while I don't know what the intent of the authors was, to me, it is simply a fun-loving tune that makes a point about life. Is one's happiness dependent on other people? That is an underlying question of the verses. I believe psychologists call that codependency. What other people think of you and feel about you is too often how you think of yourself.

There are many, many sides to happiness. The song says, "Clap along if you feel like a room without a roof." In other words, the sky's the limit. You can confine me with walls but let me reach for the stars as I move forward in life. Isn't that a part of being ordinary? Ordinary people try to do their best. And when they have done their best, there is a sense of accomplishment and satisfaction.

The *Winston Dictionary* defines *happiness* as "the state or quality of being glad or contented," "contentment," "good fortune," "good luck," "prosperity." It then continues for at least another one hundred words describing the word *happiness* and its synonyms. If you type the question "What is happiness?" in your search engine, this is what comes up: "Happiness is a mental or emotional state of well-being defined by positive or pleasant emotions ranging from contentment to intense joy. A variety of biological, psychological, religious and philosophical approaches have striven to define happiness and identify its sources."

I know there have been studies done on the happiest countries. In this one, from CNN and Columbia University's Earth Institute from 2010 to 2012, the top one was Denmark. It had much to do with their form of government and the relationships of the people. It is a fairly homogenous culture where most of the citizens seem to live in harmony with those around them since they are so very much alike. In this particular study, the next four were Norway, Switzerland, the Netherlands, and Sweden. The United States was seventeenth.

I believe, however, that happiness has less to do with what I am and more to do with who I am and who I believe myself to be in relation to those around me and, perhaps more importantly, the place of God in my worth. I have known very happy people who claimed to be atheists. I have wondered if they really were. In an online article,[2] the writer quoted a Harvard study that stretched over the course of seventy-five years. That is a long time, actually about the average lifetime of a human being. That study found that happiness and health had nothing to do with fame, money, or success. "Good relationships keep us happier and healthier. Period." The biggest results of the conclusions of the researchers were as follows: (A) People who are socially connected are happier, physically healthier and live longer. (B) Quality and quantity when it comes to close relationships are the most important. Relationship satisfaction predicts future health. (C) While high-conflict marriages can be worse than divorce, a "good relationship doesn't mean zero bickering. There are ups and downs, but trust, commitment, and respect are really the keys." (D) Loneliness kills. The feeling of loneliness can be toxic. People who are isolated are less happy, their health declines sooner as does brain function, and they live shorter lives.

The advice of the researchers is to make friends in and out of work. They go on to say, "Relationships are messy and complicated. It's not sexy or glamorous. But it's lifelong."

When I went to the country of Haiti to work on the building of a school and orphanage, I saw people who seemed to be some of the happiest people on earth. They had virtually nothing in terms of material possessions, but they had one another. The pastor of the church that was overseeing the project walked six miles one way from his home to help. He was native Haitian, and their church was housing over sixty children who had no home or family to care for them. At noon breaks, the men helping with the project would eat what little food they had and sing and pray and laugh. I wished I had known Creole. I came back to the United States with a powerful feeling of privilege and thankfulness and a deeper sense that I wanted to serve God with more intensity and faithfulness than before I went.

Embedded in the United States Declaration of Independence is the phrase "life, liberty, and the pursuit of happiness." It is often a driving force in the minds of many people as they pursue their life's work and careers. After all, it is an "unalienable right given by our Creator." It often seems, however, that the more we have, the more we want. Our need for luxury, speed, and performance is seen in cars. And the more expansive and expensive our homes, the "happier" we will be. It is, unfortunately, a carrot that the pig, or any other animal that eats carrots, can never quite gobble down. So we are left with feelings of emptiness and loneliness and unhappiness, the opposite of the very object for which we were striving.

It is also said that the happiest people on earth are those who have experienced great tragedy and fought their way through to a sense of peace and acceptance. The key is the support and encouragement of the friends and family surrounding them. The days immediately following the death of a loved one are days when neighbors and friends rally to visit. They bring food and send cards. But what happens in the weeks and months after the memorial/funeral service? The person goes to bed and wakes up alone. Yet they persevere. Those folks are the people who view themselves as students, not victims. Students learn and grow and love. Victims complain and demean and have self-pity.

The line in the song that says "Clap along if you feel that happiness is the truth" rings loud and clear to me. I want to be a seeker, not of happiness, but of truth. And in seeking truth, especially truth about life and God, happiness will follow. Psalms 42:1–2a tells us, "as the hart [deer] longs for flowing streams, so longs my soul for you, O God. My soul thirsts for God, for the living God."

---

[1] Pharrell Williams, "Happy," from the movie *Despicable Me 2* soundtrack (EMI Blackwood Music Publishing Inc. 2013).

[2] *MSN*, titled "Happiness and Health," March 24, 2016.

Chapter 4

Undeserved Forgiveness

"Amazing Grace"[1]

1. Amazing grace! How sweet the sound
That saved a wretch like me!
I once was lost, but now am found; was blind, but now I see.

2. Twas grace that taught my heart to fear,
And grace my fears relieved;
How precious did that grace appear the hour I first believed.

3. Through many dangers, toils, and snares
I have already come;
'tis grace has brought me safe thus far, and grace will lead me home.

4. The Lord has promised good to me;
His word my hope secures;
He will my shield and portion be as long as life endures.

5. When we've been there ten thousand years,
Bright shining as the sun,
We've no less days to sing God's praise than when we first begun.

Author/professor Randy Pausch, who passed away in 2008 tells a story of a time he got pulled over for speeding.[2] After giving the officer his license and registration and answering several questions, he said that the reason he was driving there at all was that he had terminal cancer and only had months to live. They exchanged polite remarks to each other since he didn't look like he was sick. Dr. Pausch finally lifted up his shirt revealing surgical scars. He finishes that chapter with these words: "The cop looked at my scars. He looked in my eyes. I could see on his face: he knew he was talking to a dying man. And if by some chance I was the most brazen con man he'd ever stopped, well, he wasn't taking this any further. He handed me back my license. 'Do me a favor,' he said, 'slow down from now on.' The awful truth had set me free. As he trotted back to his police car, I had a realization. I have never been one of those gorgeous blondes who could bat her eyelashes and get out of tickets. I drove home under the speed limit, and I was smiling like a beauty queen."

For Randy Pausch, the result of being forgiven for speeding was to willingly and joyfully drive within the speed limit and smile while doing it. In a much-larger context, isn't that what grace should do for us? Why do we push it away? Why do we continue to live in guilt and shame after being told we are forgiven and loved unconditionally by a gracious God? Is it because we like guilt for some reason? We're afraid that if we die not feeling guilty, it may impact our eternal standing. After all, don't we have guilt to keep us humble? Mac Davis sang, "O Lord, it's hard to be humble when you're perfect in every way."

One day in April, I was driving by the offices of a Christian radio station. On the outside billboard was the phrase "He's not mad at you." Why do we need to see that? Why do we need to hear that? Is it because we have become so focused on pointing out the faults of others that we can't see "the log in our own eye"? So many Christian authors have written about grace, and all of us try to understand it. I realize the dilemma. On the one hand, God expresses his displeasure with humankind. Only six chapters after we have the account of God creating humanity, he is so upset with the evil that we are doing to one another that he comes up with a plan to wipe us out. On the other hand, God listened to the cries of Noah and granted him and his family immunity from the coming catastrophe.

Sister Mary Rose McGeady details stories of the million or so homeless youth sleeping on the streets in America. The first few sentences of the first chapter in her book begins thusly: "Have you ever asked the question and not wanted an answer? Homeless kids do it all the time. One they often ask is, 'What did I do to deserve this?'"[3] They are filled with guilt. They believe the mess in their lives right now is because they deserved the abuse and neglect and abandonment and the pain they have experienced. And this translates into their understanding of God, for they believe that God also must not care. How sad.

In Matthew 19, Jesus is giving a teaching to the Pharisees who have asked him about the legality of divorce. In the middle of that chapter, we read, "Then children were brought to Him that he might lay his hands on them and pray. The disciples rebuked the people; but Jesus said, 'Let the children come to me, and do not hinder them; for to such belongs the kingdom of heaven.' And he laid his hands on them and went away."

I have a ceramic image of Jesus about eight inches high sitting on my office desk. Jesus has one arm around a little boy about two and the other around a girl about four. Nuzzling against his knee is a lamb. I look at it often. It keeps me humble. I want to be a child so God can teach me stuff.

Author and speaker Philip Yancey gives the difference between grace and what he calls ungrace. "The world runs by ungrace," he says. "Everything depends on what I do. Jesus's kingdom calls us to another way, one that depends not on our performance but his own."[4]

It was about the middle of April. I had gotten a phone call to come to the hospital. Irene had taken a turn for the worse, and her children had been called for one last time. When I arrived, it was dark, around 8:00 p.m. Irene's two daughters were waiting outside the room. Their brother was on his way from Ohio and would soon be arriving. They wanted to talk to him before he and they went in to see Mom. I introduced myself, and we made some conversation about family, their dad who had passed away several years ago, and their own lives. Their brother arrived, and since the nurses were in the room, we waited and visited. One of the daughters explained to me that her daughter had been killed in a car accident by a drunk driver just a few years ago. She had become a volunteer for the organization MADD (Mothers against Drunk Drivers). I applauded her for it and expressed my sympathy at the tragic death of her child. The brother, standing close by, said with a smile, "I'm a member of DAMM—Drunks against Mad Mothers." I was stunned and incredulous. Here was his sister telling about the sad death of her young daughter. And her brother, this girl's uncle, was mocking it with a comment like that. The conversation ended, and these two sisters were gracious enough to not respond. Could this woman, whose brother seemed callous to her grief, find peace in life as well as forgiveness toward him? For me, it was a classic example of grace. It is how their dying mother would have acted. She was a kind and gentle person.

Grace and forgiveness are inextricably linked. Grace and forgiveness are also gifts that need to be applied to our own lives. Most forgiveness must be directed at ourselves before it can be directed toward another. In one visit with a church member, the understanding of grace and forgiveness came up. She, at age sixty-nine, was married to her third husband, age seventy-two, and they were very happy together. She looked me in the eye and said that she wanted to confess something that she had never told anyone. She said, "I had an abortion when I was sixteen. It was illegal, and my parents made me do it because we were a very strict Christian family and members of a very fundamental church."

How very sad. For fifty-three years, she carried that guilt, unable to find forgiveness—not only forgiveness from a loving God, but also forgiveness for herself. I have heard it said that Christians get very angry toward other Christians who sin differently than they do. A big part of grace and forgiveness is with oneself. Believing that we are indeed created in the image of God is the best place to start. It is the only place to start.

In the 1984 movie *Places in the Heart*, the last scene is very spiritually charged. At the beginning, Royce, the sheriff, is shot and killed accidentally by a young black boy named Wylie. He is subsequently dragged through town and then hung. Sheriff Royce's widow, Edna, played by Sally Field, must work through various conflicts to keep the home place.

The story ends at a church where communion is being served. Both the living and the dead are in attendance. The last line of the film is spoken by Wylie, the young African American boy, to Royce, the sheriff that he shot. He says, "Peace of God."

A good pastor friend of mine, Morris Vaagenes, teaches grace and salvation in five steps. The first is "*You must.*" In Jesus's Sermon on the Mount in Matthew 5, 6, and 7, he teaches life principles. Blessed are the meek and the merciful and the peacemakers. At the end of chapter 6, he tells us, "You, therefore, must be perfect, as your Heavenly Father is perfect." A very tall order.

Our response is the second point: "*I can't.*" In Romans 7:15, the apostle Paul himself says, "I do not understand my own actions. For I do not do what I want, but I do the very thing I hate."

The third step is "*He did.*" In the same book of Romans, chapter 5, verse 6, we are told, "While we were still weak, at the right time Christ died for the ungodly." Great, God. Now what?

Point four is "*Please do.*" The Gospel of John, chapter 1, verse 12 tells us what to do: "But to all who received him, who believed in his name, he gave power to become children of God." Dr. Karoline Lewis, in her *John* commentary, writes, "For the Gospel of John, however, to be a child of God is a literal claim. This Gospel imagines that every single aspect of the parent-child relationship is operative in our relationship with God. Everything a child needs from a parent, for survival, protection, to be sustained and nurtured, to grow and mature—this is what God provides."[5] We serve an awesome God!

The fifth and final acknowledgement is "*Thank you.*" How can we say thanks for the things you have done for us, God (chapter 10)? "Thanks be to God for his inexpressible gift" (2 Corinthians 9:15).

The hymn "Amazing Grace" was written by a cruel slave trader named John Newton. After his conversion, he renounced slavery and worked very hard to abolish it. As my older brother Jim consistently reminds me, "TGIF, Mike. Thank God I'm forgiven." How precious did that grace appear the hour I first believed? It is in seeking God's grace and experiencing that grace that we find joy and freedom and strength.

---

[1] "Amazing Grace," written by John Newton, music by W. Walker (Southern Harmony, 1835).
[2] Randy Pausch (New York, New York: Hyperion, 2008), pg. 104.
[3] Sr. Mary Rose McGeady, *Are You Out There, God?* (Covenant House Publishers, 1996), chapter 5.
[4] Philip Yancey, *What's So Amazing about Grace?* (Zondervan Publishing House, 1997), pg. 72.
[5] Karoline Lewis, *John* (Minneapolis: Fortress Press, 2014), pg. 17.

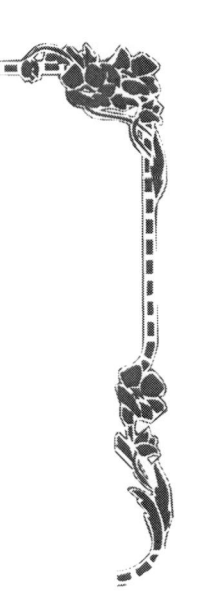

Chapter 5

Your Life's Purpose

"Nowhere Man"[1]

*1. He's a real nowhere man, sitting in his Nowhere Land
Making all his nowhere plans for nobody*

*2. Doesn't have a point of view, knows not where he's going to,
Isn't he a bit like you and me?*

*Chorus
Nowhere man, please listen, you don't know what you're missin'
Nowhere Man, the world is at your command!*

*3. He's as blind as he can be, just sees what he wants to see,
Nowhere Man can you see me at all?
Nowhere Man, don't worry, take your time, don't hurry,
Leave it all till somebody else lends you a hand.*

This song by the late John Lennon has always intrigued me. I believe it is indicative of John's search for meaning in life. I also believe it represents the cry for hope in a world that seems to have forgotten that it is purpose that motivates the average person. It is a drive to accomplish something, to leave a legacy of some sort, and to be remembered when we leave this earth. The nowhere man doesn't have a plan, has no moral center, and ignores those around him at their expense. The world is a huge and dynamic place that offers multiple opportunities to set goals and measure one's own success based on those. But alas, nowhere man simply goes through life basically surviving himself.

In the book *Growing Older and Wiser*, author Dr. Nathan Billig tells this story:[2]

> A 76-year-old, a recently retired attorney, became despondent when he realized that he "wasn't doing anything since he retired." He spent the morning reading two newspapers, taking a walk, and sometimes shopping. Twice during the week he played tennis, and he met a friend for lunch at a downtown restaurant one day each week. Since the age of 16 he had been a hard-working, striving man who always had goals, primarily school and then work oriented, that challenged him. Now he had none, and he felt useless. "I'm not doing enough," he said. After casting about for some activities of interest "that were not just busy work," he became involved in a mediation project at the city courthouse. He had responsibilities to clients and to the court but the flexible hours he wanted.

I realize men and women differ sometimes on work and how they view it. It has been said that men live for their work and women live for one another and relationships. There seems to be a little of both in all of us. Since both genders are created in the image of God, then God has placed gifts, talents, and abilities in each one of us.

This retired attorney said that he had lost a sense of future. When he made the statement that he wasn't doing anything, what he really meant was that he wasn't doing anything that mattered to the lives of people.

The brilliant scientist/mathematician Albert Einstein wrote, "Everybody is a genius. But if you judge a fish by its ability to climb a tree, it will live its whole life believing that it is stupid." So often I hear folks, especially those who are young, tell me that they don't want to try a certain skill or task because they aren't very good at it. The risk is not worth the cost if they fail. And it is failure and being embarrassed in front of others that keeps us from many of the challenges in life. We learn that trait at a young age, especially in middle and high school. And for many, that deep need to be accepted by our peers never leaves.

There are four kinds of risk. One kind is the risk you simply must take. You have no other option. A second kind of risk is one you can afford to take. You have calculated the cost, and this risk is worth it. A third one is a risk you cannot afford to take. The results of that risk would be disastrous. And the fourth is a risk you cannot afford not to take. It is a risk that takes courage and trust.

Rick Warren focused on this in his best-selling books concerning a life that is about one's purpose. He tapped into the soul of the reader in addressing the core value of who a person is and where that person gets their energy. In it he talks about why we do what we do, especially those of us who are Christians. The first sentence of the book says, "It's not about you." He explains that our life is to be about glorifying God. I will write more about that in a future chapter.

I have attended concerts by Aretha Franklin and Stevie Wonder. Both of them talk much about their appreciation for a God who has blessed them with musical abilities and talent. They really cannot help but use those gifts. Neither of them would be on the top ten list of gospel artists, but both were raised in a church. Franklin's father was a pastor, and both expressed glory to God for their success in life. Many professional athletes do the same in interviews following games.

When H. M. Stanley went to Africa in 1871 to find and report on the work of David Livingstone, he spent several months living with him. Livingstone never spoke to Stanley about religion or anything spiritual, but his loving and genuine compassion for the African people was amazing. Stanley wondered, *How could David have such love and patience for these "backward" people?* Livingstone served those whom he had no reason to love except for Christ's sake. Stanley wrote in his journal, "When I saw that unwearied patience, that unflagging zeal, and those enlightened sons of Africa, I became a Christian at his side, though he never spoke to me one word."

To be a nowhere man is to live one's life without focus and without purpose. I want to be a somewhere man. I, like you, want to leave the world a better place after I'm gone. And I will use the God-given gifts that I have to do just that, because I believe finding one's purpose and one's inner drive is a key to having the joy of the Lord.

---

[1] "Nowhere Man," written by John Lennon and Paul McCartney, performed by the Beatles from their *Rubber Soul* album, EMI Studios, London, 1965, Parlophone label.

[2] Nathan Billig, *Growing Older and Wiser* (Lexington Books, a part of Maxwell Communications, 1993).

Chapter 6

The Art of Contentment

"Come on Over"[1]

1. Make a wish-make a move
Make up your mind, you can choose
When you're up, when you're down
When you need a laugh come around
Get a life-get a grip
Get away somewhere, take a trip
Take a break, take control
Take advice from someone you know

2. Be a winner, be a star
Be happy to be who you are
Gotta be yourself, gotta make a plan
Gotta go for it while you can
Come on over, come on in
Pull up a seat-take a load off your feet
Come on over, come on in
You can unwind, take a load off your mind

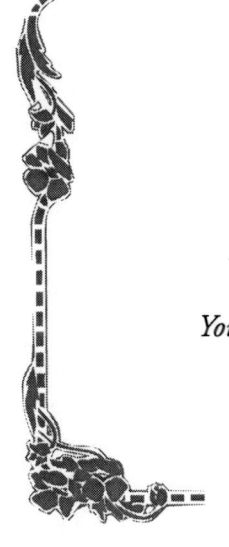

This song is one of Shania Twain's most well-known hits. It asks us to relax and take life one day at a time. It is a reminder to us that there are trials and tribulations in this life and we need to acknowledge that we get one chance at living. Bad things will happen in and to each one of us, but the negative is there only to make us strong. That is all easy to say, especially if we aren't the ones going through that particular difficulty.

Even with Jesus's disciples, there was great disillusionment. In the days following his death, they were frustrated, despondent, and disappointed. Expectations of life or situations or God can affect our faith. What happens to faith when what we expect doesn't occur? Many books have been written about suffering and failed hope. The most well-known in my experience is Harold Kushner's book *When Bad Things Happen to Good People*. It is one of the ultimate questions asked of God and the most frequently. How can a loving God see such suffering in the world and not do something about it? The question gets turned around when it is asked in a different way. How can good people see suffering in the world and not work to alleviate it?

One of my high school English teachers would always tell us not to be in the "yah but" club. He might say, "Mike, you should have done better on this test." And I might respond, "Yah but, Mr. Smith, I didn't have time to study." In today's world, there is a "right but" club as written about by sociologist Faith Popcorn. It is for people who did the right thing but life didn't work out as planned. For example, I exercised, but I still got heart disease. I took antioxidants but got cancer. I spent time studying but did poorly on a test. I worked hard but was still laid off. Ms. Popcorn says, "It shouldn't be surprising that life isn't predictable, but our consumer society, the self-help industry, and the media have all conspired to have us believe that we can actually micromanage our destinies. We are looking for a magic pill, a quick fix, or an instant solution so we can feel good, either about ourselves or those around us or our circumstances."

In the world of faith, we want the act of baptism to save us, the act of communion to forgive us, and the Bible study that we attend to cure us. I wholeheartedly believe in baptism since it is commanded in Scripture. I strongly recommend regularly receiving the

Eucharist because Jesus commanded it. And I see no downside to weekly Bible studies with other people. Perhaps our thinking about those three—and there are many more in the world of religion—is simply wrong. I have a saying that I talked about with my daughters as they were growing up. It is the words "wrong thinking." *You don't love me. This or that teacher has it in for me. The world is a bad place. I'll never amount to anything*—those thoughts and comments are simply wrong thinking.

In one of Charles Schulz's *Peanuts* comic strips, he uses Lucy to put context into a personal belief system that is wrong:

> Psychiatric Help: Five Cents, the Doctor Is In!
> Lucy says to Charlie Brown:
> "Sometimes I feel we are not communicating.
> You, Charlie Brown, are a foul ball in the line drive of life.
> You're often in the shadow of your own goalpost.
> You're three putts on the eighteenth green.
> You're a 7–10 split in the tenth frame.
> You have dropped a rod and reel in the lake of life.
> You're a called third strike.
> Do you understand? Have I made myself clear?"

The incorrect understandings of who we are reflect on how we see ourselves in relation to the universe, God, and those around us. They are meant to make us feel like we are created not in the image of God but in the image of some insignificant force that is putting pieces of a puzzle together randomly. And those pieces don't fit. A camel is a horse put together by a committee. There are times for committees, but we are not created by one. We are made by a God with a name. In Christian orthodoxy, that God has three different persons: Father, Son, and Holy Spirit. However, God is one god. And the more we allow God to be god, we see God's hand in the purposes of our lives.

I really enjoy the humorous and creative writing of authors like the late Erma Bombeck and Robert Benchley. They help me see the light side of life. Robert Benchley attended Harvard. For one class, he was assigned to write a final paper on the Anglo-American fishing dispute. Barely cracking a book much of the semester, his creative and desperate juices flowed in the essay: "I know nothing about the point of view of Great Britain in the arbitration of the international fishing problem, and nothing about the point of view of the United States. Therefore I shall discuss the question from the point of view of the fish."[2]

Over the course of my life, I have received compliments about how I handled situations, how I was as a teacher or pastor, or how my sense of humor has enabled me to go through difficulties. Many times, they are prefaced by "I don't want you to get a big head but . . ." I know the giver of the approval means well; however, isn't there something odd that when we tell someone they have done a good job, we want to make sure they don't think "too highly of themselves"? Therefore, it apparently is my job to humble a person before I give them praise. Let it not be so. Their humility or lack of it is not my responsibility.

In the short book of Philemon in the New Testament, we read about choices, affirmation, and making difficult decisions about who we are and how we live that out. The twenty-five verses center on a slave named Onesimus, meaning "useful." Under the influence of the apostle Paul, he has become a follower of Christ.

Paul truly likes Onesimus, but Paul has a dilemma of sorts. Legally the slave belongs to Philemon. And ironically, Philemon is also a follower of Christ as well as a friend of the apostle. Paul's perplexing question is, Should I send Onesimus back to Philemon as the law says? Runaway slaves could be put to death.

Some would think there is no issue. Philemon shouldn't be owning slaves in the first place. But it is not as simple as it sounds. In a society where people were property, if Philemon lets his slave go, how would he be treated by his friends who are very likely also slave owners? And what may complicate the situation even more is that some historians think that it is possible that Onesimus stole something from his owner before he left. So Philemon might have had legitimate reasons for not feeling too kindly toward this slave.

Paul wants Philemon, the slave owner, to do the right thing. He wants to give him the opportunity to make the decision for himself. Paul sends Onesimus, the slave, back to his owner with this letter called Philemon. In it he asks Philemon to welcome Onesimus back, not as a slave, but as a brother in Christ. In the letter, Paul even makes a play on the words of Onesimus's name. He writes, "Formerly he was useless to you, but now he has become useful both to you and me." His name meant "useful." Once he was useless. Now he is Onesimus, useful.

It is a wonderful story of many philosophical and theological ideas. For me, the main one of which is that Paul is asking Philemon to give Onesimus a second chance. It is the message of the cross, of redemption, of hope, and of forgiveness.

We could learn something by understanding that life is indeed too short. Live in the moment. Carpe diem. Today is a gift. Tomorrow is a promise. And I believe finding out how to accept that bit of wisdom is a part of keeping strength in the joy of the Lord.

---

[1] "Come On Over," written by Robert John Lange and Shania Twain (Universal Music Publishing, *Off the Greatest Hits* album, 1999).

[2] David Pietrusza, quoted from *A Profile in Humor* by Robert Benchley, online.

Chapter 7

God's Timing

"Turn! Turn! Turn!"[1]

(Chorus) To everything, turn, turn, turn,
There is a season, turn, turn, turn,
And a time to every purpose under heaven.

1. A time to be born, a time to die,
A Time to plant, a time to reap,
A time to kill, a time to heal,

2. A time to laugh, a time to weep,
A time to build up, a time to break down,
A time to dance, a time to mourn,
A time to cast away stones, a time to gather stones together.

3. A time of love, a time of hate,
A time of war, a time of peace,
A time you may embrace, a time to refrain from embracings,
A time to gain, a time to lose,
A time to rend, a time to sew,
A time to love, a time to hate,
A time of peace, I swear it's not too late.

When I was in my twenties, I often prayed for God's will to be done in my life. "Where should I go to college?" "Should I take this job or that job?" And there were details of life that are too numerous to mention. I wanted to be in God's will all the time. The energy spent pondering whether I should drive home twenty-four miles on a weekend to visit my family or remain in the community where I attended college would have been better spent musing about deeper issues. Such is the life of most religious young people.

As I have grown in both my chronological and spiritual age, I now believe God's timing in life is far more important than being in or out of God's will. God's will varies so much, depending on an individual's gifts, talents, and abilities, that it is truly hard to get a handle on it. And I have found that people make judgments based on being in the will of God on whether life is difficult or easy. If it is easy, God is blessing me and I must be doing what God wants. Unless one has some supernatural experience, like Mary being told by an angel she was going to give birth to a boy while she remained a virgin, finding the definitive will of God is difficult at best.

I remember when I was a teenager visiting with my dad about understanding what God wanted for my life. He talked about two wills of God: permissive and perfect. The permissive will of God are those things that happen to us that God allows but are not what God really wants, nor are they the best. The perfect will of God is more exact and precise and directed. It is one way of explaining it.

However, perhaps understanding God's timing might be a little easier and not require quite as much energy, hand-wringing, and anxiety. After I had been in my first call as a pastor for about three and a half years, as an associate, I felt like I wanted to shepherd a church by myself. Whether it was God's will or not, I didn't know, but I believed it was time for me to move on. I interviewed at a few churches, one of which was a small town parish in Wisconsin. About the same time, I visited over the phone with a senior pastor of a large Minneapolis congregation. I wanted to go there. It sounded exciting. On a Tuesday night, I received a phone call from the president of the church council in Wisconsin. He said they had decided that I was their guy, but before they actually took the time to put together a contract, he wanted to know if I would accept it.

Tom: "We are in unanimous agreement that we want you to be our pastor."
Mike: "Thank you so much! Are you sure?"
Tom: "We are sure. But we want to know if you will come before we move forward."
Mike: "Well, I guess so. Yah!"
Tom: "So you'll come to Frederic."
Mike: "Yes, I'll come."
Tom: "Great."

The next day about midmorning, I received a phone call from Harley, the senior pastor in Minneapolis.

Harley: "Mike, our committee met last night, and we'd like you to be our associate."
Mike: "Really?"
Harley: "Yes! Are you interested?"
Mike: "Harley, I would be very interested, but last night, I received a call from a church in Wisconsin and agreed to take it. I gave them my word."
Harley: "So we're too late?"
Mike: "Yes, by just a few hours."

It was a decision with very large ramifications. My oldest daughter was about four and a half, and my youngest was one. My wife was working some temporary jobs but wasn't into a career. The move would determine where my children would attend school, though we didn't know for how long. The community was about a thousand people with growth potential and expectations. It was a single church and one in which I would find some of the greatest challenges and rewards of my career. And it was all about timing. Sure, I prayed.

Mike: "Should we do this, God?"

God: "I guess so."
Mike: "What does that mean, God? Give me a dream, a vision, a confirmation of some kind, a fleece." (In Judges 6, Gideon asks God for a definite sign of his will. He put out a fleece of wool, and if there was dew on it but not on the ground, it was God's will for Israel's deliverance through Gideon.)
God: "Nope. Ain't gonna happen. Take it on faith, and we'll see down the road."

Many life changes happen in what are called defining moments, a yes-or-no answer to a question.

Man: "Will you marry me?"
Woman: "No. I'm sorry." Or "Yes, I love you." (The man and woman's role could certainly be reversed.)

The decision to pursue what one believes to be God's will for one's life can be influenced by factors such as pride, selfishness, greed, or arrogance. Maybe the image we have of ourselves is so marred by childhood trauma we don't have the confidence to listen to the still, small voice of God or even know what it sounds like. If our ego is such that hearing God is not possible, then how can we know God's will?

Author Dan Schaeffer relates a study found in the February 19, 1996, edition of *Psychological Review*. A team had studied crime and aggression and found virtually no evidence linking violence to low self-image. "Instead, researchers concluded that high self-esteem (pride) might be the culprit, especially when a person with an inflated ego feels threatened. Roy Bauermeister of Ohio's Case Western Reserve University said, 'Does anyone really think that the cause of world peace would be promoted if we boosted Saddam Hussein's self-esteem?' (This was written before his fall and death.) He concluded, perhaps it would be better to try instilling modesty and humility."[2]

There are many articles written addressing one's age as it relates to timing and accomplishments. Is there life after fifty? For example, at age fifty-three, Margaret Thatcher became Britain's first female prime minister. At seventy-two, Golda Meir became prime minister of Israel. At seventy-seven, astronaut and Senator John Glenn participated in a mission to space. At eighty, Grandma Moses, who had started painting in her late seventies, had her first one-woman exhibit. At eighty, Benjamin Franklin skillfully mediated between disagreeing factions at the US Constitutional Convention. And on his one hundredth birthday, ragtime pianist Eubie Blake exclaimed, "If I'd known I was going to live this long, I'd have taken better care of myself."

A case study of timing in life would be the story of Joseph in the book of Genesis. He has dreams and visions of future events. His father loves him more than his brothers, which makes their hatred of him even more intense. So as to be spared death by those same brothers, he is sold as a slave to a traveling group of traders on their way to Egypt. Through a series of occurrences, the guy actually prospers in Egypt. Talk about making lemonade out of lemons. He is made the head over the household of Potiphar, one of Pharaoh's officers. Potiphar's wife frames him for sexual assault, for which he is imprisoned. Even while in prison, he prospers, correctly interpreting dreams for people. He becomes second in authority in Egypt just below Pharaoh himself. God used him in mighty and powerful ways to further the work of the kingdom, both God's and humankind's. And even though this was the early days of those four hundred years of slavery for the Israelite people, in the big picture, the faithfulness of God is seen time and time again.

As the writer of Ecclesiastes says, there is a time for most everything in life. Each of us is given freedom and choices and the mind to decide. But just as important as what we do is when it is done. I believe understanding the timing of God is a big part of keeping the joy of the Lord.

---

[1] "Turn! Turn! Turn!" adaptation and music by Pete Seeger in 1959, TRO Inc., sung and made famous by the group the Byrds in 1965.
[2] Dan Schaeffer, *Defining Moments* (Discovery House Publishing, 2006), pg. 48.

Chapter 8

Goals, Dreams, and Risks

"The Impossible Dream"[1]

To dream the impossible dream
To right the unbeatable foe
To bear with unbearable sorrow
To run where the brave dare not go.
To right the unrightable wrong
To love pure and chaste from afar
To try when your arms are too weary
To reach the unreachable star.
This is my quest to follow that star
No matter how hopeless, no matter how far
To fight for the right without question or pause
To be willing to march into hell for a heavenly cause
And I know if I'll only be true to this glorious quest
That my heart will lie peaceful and calm
When I'm laid to my rest.
And the world will be better for this
That one man, scorned and covered with scars
Still strove with his last ounce of courage
To reach the unreachable star.

The goal of dreams and hopes for each person, as well as the ability and gumption to leave the world a better place when we're gone, is at the heart of this song and for this ordinary man. There is no magic solution or quick way to find it. Once we have established the fact in our lives that we will have shelter, food, and clothes, we can then look forward to what is in our future. Hope, as I have talked about in other chapters, is so important in how we approach our life and goals.

In the drama for which this song was written, first titled *I, Don Quixote* and later renamed *Man of La Mancha*, the main character ignores reality to battle large objects as though they were his enemies. He, Don Quixote, is ridiculed and mocked for being an idealist, so much so that he consistently has to defend his sanity.

It seems in life, it is often the people who "live on the edge" who make a difference. They are the ones willing to take risks, venture into what is unknown, and shake up the status quo. If people were separated into two groups, explorers and settlers, they are the former. They are pioneers who travel to lands unknown. They explore territory or water upon which there has been no travel. Why do people climb mountains? Because they are there. Why do others jump out of perfectly flying airplanes at ten thousand feet? Because they can. And there are those who tie a bungee cord to their ankles and leap off a cliff. It is a thrill, a challenge to death, the ability to test limits and experience excitement that few are courageous or crazy enough to try.

A church bishop often visited a small religious college to talk to the students.[2] On one trip, he was having a conversation with the president of the college. The bishop said that the millennium could not be long in coming since everything about nature had been discovered and all possible inventions had been made. The college president disagreed with that assessment and said he felt that the next fifty years would bring amazing discoveries. Furthermore, he told the bishop human beings would be "flying through the skies like birds within a relatively short time."

"Nonsense," vociferously said the bishop. "Flight is reserved for angels!"

The bishop's name was Wright. He had two sons named Orville and Wilbur. Fortunately, for the world, the sons did not share their father's opinions about creativity, risk, or the idea that everything about nature had been discovered.

Martin Luther King's "I Have a Dream" speech looks at the world of possibilities, not as the world as it presently exists. It is the challenge of hope when there seems to be none. Perhaps Dr. King had in mind a verse from Proverbs 29 in the Bible that says, "Where there is no vision, the people are unrestrained" (NAS). Purpose and goals unite. Lawlessness occurs in a world of anarchy. Behavior that takes no one else into account other than each person's agenda and motivation will eventually wear itself out.

Companies, organizations, and churches have been told to formulate a mission statement. In a few words, usually around twelve to fifteen, committees or boards come up with a sentence that gives the purpose of the particular group. Companies have target demographics. For example, some businesses market to millennials—those born between the years 1983 and 2000. Others want to sell to generation X—those born between 1965 and 1983. And still others aim at children or baby boomers. Those parameters give vision and focus to the product or service that is being offered.

One of the clergy I got to know during my time as a pastor in Iowa was named John, and he had just resigned from his church of many years because he was sixty-five and planning on retiring. His last pastoral act was to co-officiate a funeral with the man who was taking over as shepherd for that congregation. It was a Tuesday, and the funeral was at eleven o'clock in the morning with lunch following. About suppertime that evening, I received a phone call from the senior pastor of my church informing me that John had passed away that afternoon. That evening, I went to see his wife at their home. When I asked what happened, she told me she had come home from work about 5:00 p.m. and found him sitting in his recliner deceased. It was determined to be natural causes. His heart had simply stopped beating. His purpose had ended.

Lincoln's Gettysburg Address is written in 1863 for the consecration of the national cemetery there. Interestingly enough, this 273-

word oration followed a two-hour speech given by the Honorable Edward Everett. The speech begins with the line "Four score and seven years ago." But the last sentence, which is emphasizing freedom for all people, says:

> *It is rather for us to be here dedicated to the great task of remaining before us—that from these honored dead we take increased devotion to that cause for which they gave the last full measure of devotion—that we may highly resolve that these dead shall not have died in vain. And that this nation, under God, shall have a new birth of freedom. And that government of the people, by the people, and for the people, shall not perish from the earth.*

We truly need to live our lives with purpose and direction. It is difficult. It is painful at times. Can we be true to what we were created to be and do? We compare ourselves to others as if that validates our own existence. It may in part, but after all is said and done, who we are and what we strive for is the legacy that we leave.

I have been in workshops where we are asked to think of our own personal mission statement. A question we had to answer was, "If you had five minutes at halftime of the Super Bowl, what would you say?" Another way of putting it is this: "What is at the core of your being that gets you up and going in the morning? What motivates you to go on with life?" It is a question that becomes more and more important as we age. Why is suicide increasing in the over-seventy age bracket, especially among males? Have they given up? Has the remote control on the television become more important than their relationships with their spouses, families, and friends? Because we are living longer and leading more active lives, these issues become more central. At one of my last doctor visits for my annual physical, he said that about half of illnesses and issues in the older population can be attributed to a lack of activity and exercise.

One of my eighty-five-year-old former church members told me three days before he died, "Pastor Mike, we live until we die. And then we die." He went from the hospital to a care center and lived there one day.

The connection between joy and energy is often apparent. I admire those who keep their sense of humor while facing "giants." They inspire me to continue the work of loving people and serving the world to make it a better place. They encourage me to look forward for finding my place in this journey and not in the past. I have peace that the strength in me originates in the hope of my loving, heavenly Father.

---

[1] Joe Darian, "The Impossible Dream," music composed by Mitch Leigh (published by Sam Fox Publishing Company Inc. 1967).

[2] Nido Qubein, *Get the Best from Yourself* (Prentice Hall Trade, 1983).

Chapter 9

Eternity

"I Can Only Imagine"[1]

I can only Imagine
I can only imagine what it will be like
When I wake up by your side
I can only imagine what my eyes will see
When your face is before me.
Surrounded by your glory, what will my heart feel?
Will I dance for you, Jesus or in awe of you be still?
Will I stand in your presence or to my knees will I fall?
Will I sing Hallelujah, will I be able to speak at all?
I can only imagine when that day comes.
When I find myself standing in the Son.
I can only imagine when all I would do is forever,
Forever worship you.
I can only imagine.

Donna caught me after church one Sunday informing me she had been diagnosed with cancer. I expressed my dismay and asked if she wanted to visit about it sometime this week. She came in to the office Tuesday morning during a lunch break from work. She had gone to the doctor a week ago because she thought she had a bad case of the flu. She got worse by the hour and returned to her physician. After a series of tests, it was determined she had cancer, stage 4. Some people beat it, and she might too.

She updated me weekly on her progress with chemotherapy and a regimen of diet and exercise. At her six-week checkup, this fifty-year-old mother and grandmother was given less than three weeks to live. The cancer had spread.

On Saturday, November 3, she slipped into a coma. She was living at home under the guidance of hospice with her family around her. I received a phone call about five o'clock on Sunday morning informing me she had passed away and asking if I could come to the house. On the way, I turned my radio on to a Christian station. The song that was playing was "I Can Only Imagine." I used it along with Scripture as a basis for my sermon at her funeral a few days later.

In a story on one of the morning news shows in December 2016, the reporter was asking a person who had had a near-death experience what changed in her life. Her immediate response: "I no longer fear death, and that has allowed me to live my life with a greater appreciation and freedom than I had known before."

Imagination gives us opportunities to escape reality, even if for short periods of time. We can go to places in the world that we haven't visited if we picture in our minds what we might see there, especially if we have viewed pictures. It can also give us the stuff nightmares are made of. We imagine being assaulted in our sleep because of stories we have heard on the news about people doing bad things.

In 1 Corinthians 2 in the Bible, the apostle Paul writes, "But it is written, what no eye has seen, nor ear heard, nor the heart of humankind has conceived, what God has prepared for those who love him." In the same book in chapter 15, Paul addresses death: "For this perishable nature must put on the imperishable, and this mortal nature must put on immortality. When the perishable puts on the imperishable, and the mortal puts on immortality, then shall come to pass the saying that is written: 'Death is swallowed up in victory. O death, where is your victory? O death, where is your sting?' The sting of death is sin, and the power of sin is the law. But thanks be to God who gives us the victory through our Lord Jesus Christ."

The truth of these passages and believing and experiencing them can be two different things. When a child dies, we ask the question about the fairness of life. Why did God let this happen? Couldn't God have healed him/her? How could God let this freak accident happen? Why do bad things happen to good people? Those are the most asked questions by people of all backgrounds. The answer is elusive. We want to know, but those "why" answers cannot be understood, at least not in this side of eternity.

Lyle and Louise were business owners. Louise came to worship more often than Lyle. One reason was that their business required them to work early mornings, including Sundays. So I got to know them mostly from frequenting their place of work.

Lyle and Louise had two children, a boy and a girl. Bradley, the son, was thirty-one and married. The daughter, Sharon, was twenty-three and soon to be married. Life was good for Lyle and Louise. Sharon and her husband didn't have any children, but Bradley and his wife had two young boys. Louise often talked about the grandsons and how quickly they were growing.

On Sunday morning, July 25, 1999, immediately following the second worship service, one of Louise's sisters informed me that Sharon had suddenly passed away while bear hunting that very morning. I couldn't believe it. She was only thirty-one. Her eleven-year-old nephew had been along and was by her side. It was a massive heart attack. I left for Lyle and Louise's home to see if there was anything I could do. Sharon's funeral was Thursday of that week.

It was difficult, but Lyle and Louise had their son and grandsons. Their homes were less than a mile apart. The oldest grandson would be starting confirmation the next fall. I would then get to know him and the family better in the discussions that we always had in class. We all thought it would be therapeutic for the grandson to

THE JOY OF THE LORD IS MY STRENGTH

have a positive understanding of God and be able to share thoughts of his aunt in a safe environment with the other students.

On Saturday, September 23, 2000, the phone in my office rang. I was told that forty-year-old Bradley was bear hunting and had a massive heart attack and died on the side of the road. His son was with him at the time, the same youngster who had witnessed the sudden death of his dad's sister. In fourteen months, Lyle and Louise had lost their two children.

At both funeral services, I used John 14:1–6 as my sermon text. It is the story of Thomas asking Jesus about life, the ways of life, the meaning of life, and who he really is. I believe it is a question that all humanity could be asking. Those certainly were the thoughts of all that community during those months following Bradley's and Sharon's passing.

It is the hope of all to leave a legacy. And it is that hope that moves us forward. Death certainly has a sting. Most people sense it deep in their souls. It is a fear or an anxiety. We may not name it or ever think about it, but it is there. And we especially don't want to die alone. Perhaps that fear is even greater than the fear of the end.

A very inspiring song that I love is the theme song from the Broadway musical *Carousel*. It is titled "You'll Never Walk Alone."[2] One line tells me that there is a golden sky at the end of the storm. And the chorus says, "Walk on, walk on, with hope in your heart, and you'll never walk alone. You'll never walk alone."

While that song wasn't written to encourage a person approaching the end of their earthly journey or necessarily as a Christian admonition, it certainly addresses how to approach life. As I have told many people during a prayer with the family before we enter the sanctuary at a funeral or memorial service, there is a price to pay for loving someone. And that price is that we miss them when they are gone. If we go through life never loving people and rarely caring about others, we are protected from pain, but life is truly our loss.

When a woman named Mother Hale died in New York City, the service at Riverside Church was overflowing. Mother Hale is known as a mother to the abandoned. The people in the congregation included street people, addicts, CEOs of major corporations, the mayor, the governor, priests, and rabbis. They all came to pay their respects to this woman who touched the world with a gift, the gift of mothering.

The great running back Walter Payton was asked at a news conference prior to his death from cholangiocarcinoma (bile duct cancer) if he was scared of dying, his immediate response was, "You're damn right I am." And he was a religious man, a Christian man.

There are those who have had a spiritual experience in which they float above the body and look down at the people around them. It often takes place in a house of worship during a time of prayer after the service. Pastors in mainline churches and those very educated with doctoral degrees have lived these. They explain that they had never felt such total and complete peace, being fully conscious and aware of what was happening. According to them, God was revealing what death will be like.

The dying process is also important to understand. Hospice, an organization that works with terminally ill people, has done much to further the research and thoughts concerning the last months and weeks of one's life here on this earth. In the article "Gone from My Sight," details are given to help both the patient and the caregiver(s) better grasp what is happening. The processing of one's life is usually done with the eyes closed, so sleep increases. Words are seen as being connected with the physical life that is being left behind. They lose their importance. Touch and wordlessness take on more meaning. Focus is changing from this world to the next.

How we approach death is going to depend upon our fear of life and how much we participated in that life. It is also affected by how willing we are to let go of this known expression to venture into a new one. Fear and unfinished business are two big factors in determining how much resistance we put into meeting death.

Anne Graham Lotz tells about a missionary named Samuel Morrison, who, after twenty-five years in Africa, returned home to die. In the chapter titled "Hope When You Are Defeated by Death," she recounts Morrison's thoughts:[3]

> As it so happened, he traveled home on the same ocean liner that brought President Teddy Roosevelt

back from a hunting expedition. When the great ship pulled into New York harbor, the dock . . . was jammed with what looked like the entire population of New York City! Bands were playing, banners were waving, choirs of children were singing, multicolored balloons were floating in the air, flashbulbs were popping, and newsreel cameras were poised to record the return of the president.

Mr. Roosevelt stepped down the gangplank to thunderous cheers and applause, showered with confetti and ticker tape . . .

At the same time, Samuel Morrison quietly walked off the boat. No one was there to greet him. He slipped alone through the crowd. Because of the crush of people there to welcome the president, he couldn't even find a cab. Inside his heart, he began to complain. *Lord, the president has been in Africa for three weeks, killing animals, and the whole world turns out to welcome him home! I've given twenty-five years of my life in Africa, serving you, and no one has greeted me or even knows I'm here.*

In the quietness of his heart, a gentle, loving voice whispered, *But my dear child, you are not home yet!*

The song with which I began this chapter asks the intriguing question about what one will do when one stands before one's Creator. We won't need faith after we leave this earth because the closeness of God will be reality. There will be no need to argue and discuss issues beyond this life because all will be revealed, at least all that we will need to know. I wish there was more in the Bible about what happens after death. But for now, we have the word of people who have stories of otherworldly experiences. And they are talking and writing. And we have the Scriptures. So we keep our peace. We continue to look up and look forward. It is the hope of eternity and that joy by which we are strengthened.

---

[1] Bert Millard, "I Can Only Imagine" (Music Services Inc., sung by MercyMe, INO Records, 1999, M2.O Communications).

[2] Oscar II Hammerstein and Richard Rodgers, "You'll Never Walk Alone" (Peermusic Publishing, Imagen Music, Inc.).

[3] Anne Graham Lotz, *The Vision of His Glory* (Nashville, TN: Thomas Nelson, 1996).

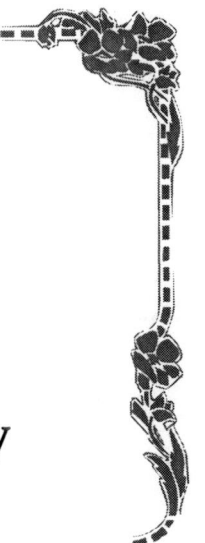

Chapter 10

To God be the Glory

"My Tribute"[1]

1. How can I say thanks for the things you have done for me?
Things so undeserved that you gave to prove your love for me.
The voices of a million angels could not express my gratitude.
All that I am and ever hope to be I owe it all to thee.

Chorus: To God be the glory
For the things he has done.
With his blood he has saved me.
With his power he has raised me.
To God be the glory for the things he has done.

2. Just let me live my life,
Let it be pleasing, Lord, to thee.
And should I gain any praise
Let it go to Calvary.

The *Westminster Shorter Catechism*, the main teaching tool of the Presbyterian Church and others, begins with a question, What is the chief end of humankind? The answer: to glorify God and enjoy him forever.

Those of you who are baseball fans may remember the name Orel Hershiser. When he was at his best, he played for the Los Angeles Dodgers. In 1988, he earned the Cy Young award as the best pitcher in baseball as well as two MVP awards, one for the National League Championship Series and one for the World Series.

During the national league play-offs, the TV cameras zoomed in on him in the dugout singing to himself. They couldn't make out what he was singing, but they knew that is what he was doing.

After the World Series was over, Mr. Hershiser was on the *Tonight Show*, which at that time was hosted by Johnny Carson. Carson asked him to sing that song right then and there on the show. With embarrassed reluctance, he sang the song: "Praise God from who all blessings flow, praise him all creatures here below. Praise him above ye heavenly host. Praise Father, Son, and Holy Ghost."

The incarnation of Christ was and is so unbelievable to many people. His bodily resurrection is a point of contention in some theological circles. For the disciples to touch him following his death on the cross and subsequent reappearance can't be underestimated. The dialogue with Thomas in the Gospel of John, chapter 20, is paramount to the salvation story of Christ. He wanted to put his own fingers into Jesus's side and hands.

Touch is imperative for our own healthy development. It even affects pain control in our physical bodies. A four-year-old became frightened during a thunderstorm. The lightning and thunder became too much for her, and she flew out of her bed and ran to her parents' room, jumping in the middle.

"I'm scared," she cried. Both parents reassured her that the Lord would protect her.

After briefly thinking about that, she replied, "I know that, but right now I need someone with skin on."

God understood that we needed someone with skin on. Some worship idols. That is skin in a way. The Hebrew people were laughed at and mocked for worshipping the invisible god. "Where is your god?" they were asked. "Show us. We want to see that god."

When I was five years old, I hurt myself while playing outside. We lived on a farm in rural southwest Minnesota, and it wasn't unusual to get a cut, scrape, abrasion, or broken bone. I remember running into the house crying. My mother, a stay-at-home mom, was busy in the kitchen. When she saw me, she picked me up, took me to a rocking chair, and simply held me and consoled me until the bleeding stopped and the pain subsided.

Now in my sixties, I recall that incident as an affirmation that my parents had my back: "Life would be OK." "You will try and fail." "We will support you." "You will experience struggles." "We will nurture you as best we can."

I had the opportunity to attend the funeral of a friend of mine, a black fellow. The service was in a predominantly African American church. Every part of that celebration of life could have been in any of the churches I had pastored. All the words of the music, the Scripture readings, and the sermon would have been appropriate for any Christian community. The only difference was that the elements of the service were done with more emotion and passion with regular responses of "Amen," "Praise the Lord," and "Hallelujah" from members of the congregation.

In the message, the pastor had four points. The first one was *invitation*. God invites each of us to receive the salvation and forgiveness that is offered in the person of Jesus Christ given out of God's love for all humankind. His words were "God invites all people to come. Not just black people. Not just Jewish people. All people."

His second point was *proclamation*. After we receive Christ into our lives, we are called to be servants of God's love. It is out of that love that we proclaim our joy and peace to the world. He said, "God uses us to bring God's love to everyone around us. It is us who people associate with God because we carry Christ's name."

The third point was *culmination*. When our lives are over, we receive eternal life promised in Jesus Christ. "It is that hope that keeps us encouraged and faithful," he preached.

The fourth and final point and the one that struck me as a wonderful promise was *coronation*. A coronation is the act of crowning a king or a queen. It occurs everywhere from high schools choosing a homecoming king and queen to Great Britain and Scandinavia crowning royalty.

There are places in the book of Revelation in which we are given the promise of receiving a crown after death. I especially like the passage from 1 Peter 5:4: "And when the chief Shepherd is manifested you will obtain the unfading crown of glory."

"Really? You mean, God, that I will be the center of a coronation ceremony?"

And God answers, "Yes, my child. My son, Jesus, will stand in front of you and place a crown on your head for your willingness to give glory to me in your life. By simply trusting and believing in me, you too will receive a crown of life" (Revelation 2:10).

In Nehemiah, chapter 8, the walls of the city of Jerusalem have just been completed, yet there is something lacking. Life is more than just brick and mortar. The lives of the Israelites are still in distress. Even though the building is completed, the people realize something is missing. In the course of being held captive in a foreign land, they had forgotten their spiritual heritage. And more than that, they had simply forgotten God. They have experienced the destructive results of rebellion and neglect.

In verse 9, Nehemiah, Ezra, and the Levites read from the law and declare the day holy. They instruct the people not to cry. The people are made aware that God has a wonderful message of salvation and that it is in his joy that they will find strength to put their lives back together. And so in verse 10, we read, "Go your way, eat the fat and drink sweet wine and send portions to him for whom nothing is prepared; for this day is holy to our Lord; and do not be grieved, for the joy of the Lord is your strength."

To God indeed be the glory for the wonderful things he has done.

---

[1] Andrae Crouch, *My Tribute* (EMI Christian Music Publishing, 1971).

About the Author

Mike Soppeland has been a Lutheran pastor in Iowa, Wisconsin, and Minnesota for over thirty years. He graduated from Southwest State University in Marshall, Minnesota, in 1976 and earned his masters of divinity degree in 1986 from Luther Theological Seminary in St. Paul, Minnesota.

He taught school for six years prior to seminary, where he also coached various sports.

He has been or is a son, brother, husband, father, teacher, pastor, and friend. He has written hundreds of articles for his church newsletters as well as newspapers. He has served on boards and committees too numerous to mention. His first book, *The Weary Pilgrim*, was published in 2016.

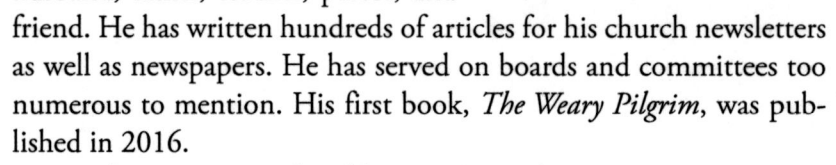

Mike is semiretired and lives in St. Paul, Minnesota.